Hiding an Elephant

Hiding an Elephant

Living With Adult ADHD

Kim A. Gay

TATE PUBLISHING & Enterprises

This book is designed to provide accurate and authoritative information with regard to the subject matter covered. This information is given with the understanding that neither the author nor Tate Publishing, LLC is engaged in rendering legal, professional advice. Since the details of your situation are fact dependent, you should additionally seek the services of a competent professional.

The opinions expressed by the author are not necessarily those of Tate Publishing, LLC.

Published by Tate Publishing & Enterprises, LLC
127 E. Trade Center Terrace | Mustang, Oklahoma 73064 USA
1.888.361.9473 | www.tatepublishing.com

Tate Publishing is committed to excellence in the publishing industry. The company reflects the philosophy established by the founders, based on Psalm 68:11,
"The Lord gave the word and great was the company of those who published it."

Published in the United States of America
ISBN: 978-1-61663-433-9
1. Self-Help / General
2. Self-Help / Personal Growth / General
10.05.18

Dedication

I would like to dedicate this book to my children, Rob, Joe, and Elly, for giving me a reason to keep trying; my best friend, Michelle, for always being there when I needed her; my mother, Judy, for more reasons than I could ever begin to mention, and my father, Fred, for the many times he said, "you can do that."

Table of Contents

Introduction

Have you ever wondered why you can't seem to get anywhere in life? Do you find yourself jumping from one job to another and end up feeling like a quitter? Are you unorganized and your valuable time is eaten up because you can't find anything? At the end of the day, which list is longer; the things you got started, or the things you finished?

Although everyone feels unorganized or frustrated from time to time, people with Attention Deficit Hyperactivity Disorder (ADHD) seem to make a career out of it. Maybe not a career by choice, but one they are compelled to follow. Studies seem to show that it is not just any career either ... it is a family business.

If you are an adult with an ADHD child and you think that you may have it too; you might be right. It appears to be very genetic. It was my son's diagnosis that led me to be tested and diagnosed, and later to the diagnosis of my daughter. After learning about the disorder, I have made informal diagnoses of some of my older family members as well. It would seem that ADHD has become more and more "popular" if you will. It is as though everyone and his brother has it. Although I think that ADHD has always been around, it is societal changes that have caused its symptoms to be more noticeable and disruptive.

Once a child with ADHD is thrust into adulthood, the whole dynamics of the disorder begin to change. They no longer have someone instructing them on what to do and how to do it. If they are unaware of their condition and how to treat it, the decisions they make can be devastating to their future as well as their self-esteem. While everyone has certain aspects of their personal life that they prefer to keep tucked away in the privacy of their own home, those with ADHD may have a difficult time accomplishing that. My poor decisions began to stand out like a sore thumb and I felt like everyone could see my failures and erratic life choices. I knew something was wrong with me, I just didn't know what. I believed that this problem I had became the "elephant in the room" that everyone noticed but nobody was addressing: at least not to me. I spent all of my energy trying to make it look like I had it all together. When that didn't work, I began cutting myself off from society. If I couldn't get rid of the elephant, I would hide it instead.

In this book, I hope to help you better understand what ADHD is and how it can affect a person even into their adult years. I want to show you how it isn't just a curse that a person has to submit to. ADHD has certain perks that many people aren't even aware of. If used for good instead of evil, a person's life and the lives of those around them can be enhanced by this so-called disorder. I'll try not to get too wordy or scientific and just get to the point. And with that point … let's begin.

Insight into ADHD

The Suspicion

Although I would rather not be a poster child for the ADHD cause, I can at least explain my own experience with it and you can look for similarities with yourself. This is how I came to the conclusion that I might have Attention Deficit Hyperactivity Disorder: most commonly known as ADHD. I was watching a morning news program and one of their guests was a woman who was diagnosed with ADHD in her mid-thirties. I heard her story and made several connections with my own life.

My son was diagnosed with ADHD after he was held back in the first grade. I had heard that it could be genetic and thought that he got it from me, because I had always had a hard time sitting still and concentrating. I had no idea before I saw this woman on the news, that so many different areas of a person's life could be affected by ADHD. I also hadn't realized that it could continue so far into adulthood.

I looked back at my life and evaluated the path that I had taken... as winding as it was. After high school, I moved from my small hometown in Michigan's Upper Peninsula to Toledo, Ohio. I was looking for a change and some independence and I had some friends there. That lasted for three months. I moved home and got a job.

A year later, I started attending a local college. I didn't quite make it through three quarters, taking classes such as Child Development, Geography of Asia, and Outdoor Survival. I couldn't decide on a major, so I quit. I didn't drop anything or talk to any of my instructors. Instead of getting an incomplete for each class, which is what I assumed would happen, I failed them.

Highlights of the next twenty years or so included a couple of unplanned pregnancies, which resulted in a couple of rushed marriages, and two divorces. I also had a dozen or more different jobs, none of which lasted more than two years, and I moved approximately twenty times. I always had good excuses for quitting or leaving; or so I thought. For the most part, I was just restless.

These events are all external signs that people could see, letting them know that something wasn't quite right with me; the "elephant in the room" so to speak. I haven't even begun to cover the internal things that come about as a result of living with the failures that I have experienced. I felt that people started to look at me differently. I got so tired of being asked, "So where are you working these days?" or "Are you still living in the same place?" I was already so ashamed of myself, that it killed me just to know that other people noticed. I got to the point where I would duck behind shelves at the grocery store to avoid talking to people who might ask a lot of questions. Eventually, I went out of the house as little as possible and would never invite anybody to come to my home, other than my best friend. I was determined to hide this elephant that had taken over my life.

I spent hours going through things, throwing away, or reorganizing them. I would tell my friend "everything is so unorganized." She said she couldn't see what I meant. Even if the house was clean and looked organized, I always felt like I was just one step away from having it all fall apart. If I didn't stay on top of it, it would become overwhelming.

I wasn't always like that. I spent many years trudging through piles of stuff left lying around. Things would get lost or broken and I would get frustrated. That frustration is what led to my need for structure and the stress that goes along with trying to achieve it. I became obsessed with having things in place.

Associated Conditions

This seems like an appropriate time to mention the other disorders that can come along in conjunction with ADHD. The struggle of having to deal with this condition, especially if undiagnosed or not properly treated, can lead to a person developing other conditions as well. When I started looking for information on ADHD, the word "co-morbid" kept popping up. I looked the word up at medterms.com, and basically, co-morbidity is when a person has two or more diagnosed conditions at the same time. It isn't uncommon for a person with ADHD to have one or more other disorders. Adults are known to have more than children. I would have to presume that this is because adults have been dealing with it longer so they have had more time to develop others. It could also be attributed to the advancement of treatments and knowledge in the area of ADHD in recent years that children are benefiting from. Some of the more common disorders associated with ADHD are:

- OCD (Obsessive Compulsive Disorder)
- Substance Abuse
- Bipolar Disorder
- Anxiety
- Sleep Disorders
- Depression
- Learning Disabilities

The problem with co-morbidity is that it is hard to tell if the ADHD has caused the other disorder, or if it stands on its own. It can also be a dilemma as to which should be treated first or to treat them simultaneously, as not all treatments go well together. This is where I am glad that I am not a doctor. Trying to figure out cause and effect can keep going around in circles and get very confusing. It is so important to have a doctor who listens to you and who you feel comfortable with. It could take awhile to set up a plan that works.

My problems started to multiply when I became obsessed with attempting to stay organized, but was unable to do so. I hadn't been diagnosed with ADHD yet, so I couldn't understand why I was having such a difficult time. I got to the point where I wouldn't even attempt to do something if I knew I wasn't going to be able to do it perfectly. Since the chance of my doing everything perfectly was not possible, a lot of things didn't get done at all.

To make matters worse, I didn't want anyone to see how imperfect things in my life were, which meant keeping people away from my house. This can be a lot more difficult than one might think. Any time we socialize with people, we open ourselves up to having someone pop over for a visit. This meant I had to keep others at a distance at all times.

The more people focus on the problems that they have, the bigger those problems can become. My simple inability to stay organized turned into a fear of being around people. I managed to do what I needed to do outside of the home. I would go to work and do my job without letting anyone get too close. I eventually quit my job and started doing private housekeeping instead. I went to these homes while everyone was gone for the day. The door would be unlocked when I arrived and they would leave a check on the table. This allowed me to have even less involvement with people.

My children's social lives required me to go to activities that they were involved in. While attending these functions, I managed to keep to myself for the most part. I would try to deter them from having a lot of friends over as well. If they wanted to go to a friend's house, I would make sure that I did the drop-offs and pick-ups to avoid the possibility of anyone coming to my door: or worse yet, wanting to come inside.

I remember the point where I realized just how bad this fear of having people come to my home had gotten. I had to purchase renter's insurance in order to keep my cat. The housing authority that I was renting from required it of all pet owners to cover liability in case someone was injured by the animal. I was told by the insurance company that they would be sending a photographer out to take pictures of the outside of the home. They wanted to make sure that it was safe and secure. I told the woman I spoke with that the housing authority had very strict guidelines for their residences and they maintained them regularly. I told her to contact my landlord if they had any questions about this. I really didn't want anyone coming to my home and probably sounded quite suspicious when I was trying to convince her not to send anyone out. I was eventually assured by her that there shouldn't be a need for that after all.

Several days later, the photographer arrived at my door. I was completely caught off guard. I kept telling him that I was told he wouldn't have to do this. I was very upset and he probably wondered what the big deal was all about. I immediately called the insurance company while he walked around outside taking pictures. It really didn't matter to me that he was taking pictures of the outside of my home. My house looked just like the rest of the houses on my street. The lease required that nothing was to be left in the yard and the grass had to be kept mowed. This was all as it should be. What bothered me was that he came to my door: that I had to open my door to this person.

I yelled at the woman on the phone. Of course, I couldn't admit to her that I had this phobia. I had to make up some excuse for my anger. I ranted on about how it made no sense for them to pay someone to come all the way up from Detroit to take pictures when there was no reason for it. No wonder their insurance cost so much, since they were requiring these unnecessary expenses. I immediately cancelled my insurance.

The day wasn't over yet though. Shortly after the photographer left, while I was still in a panic, there was another knock at the door. I had some mail that wouldn't fit in the box, so the mail carrier wanted to hand it to me personally. Luckily, I didn't make a scene this time. After I took my mail from him, I shut the door and broke down. I screamed into a pillow so the neighbors wouldn't hear. I felt so unbelievably out of control.

Even now, after being diagnosed with ADHD, some of the new disorders that I developed out of the frustration of not knowing what was wrong with me still linger. The anxiety I feel over having people step into my home has not completely gone away. I still like a heads up when someone is coming over and some major time to prepare myself and my home. I realize this is not "normal" and that other people really don't care what my house looks like. All of that doesn't matter ... because I care.

How Did This Get Missed?

Many adults missed being diagnosed as children. Sometimes there aren't any outward signs, like the typical disruptive behavior, to tip parents and teachers off, so it may be assumed that a child has a general learning disorder instead. In girls, often times their inattentiveness is blamed on a preoccupation with boys, or just plain daydreaming.

Occasionally a child is so intelligent and works so hard to compensate for their symptoms that a disorder isn't even suspected. The adults in their life may not sense the amount of anxiety and effort they go through just trying to keep up. ADHD doesn't determine how intelligent a person is; rather intelligence and perseverance may determine how well a person will handle their ADHD. Treatment shouldn't be deemed unnecessary just because they are holding their own. The intense pace they are keeping could eventually push them over the edge.

Besides the common practice of people trying to hide their problems rather than dealing with them, another reason that ADHD may be missed in women is because they are often quickly diagnosed with depression and the search ends there. Even if it were decided that the depression was caused by the circumstances they were dealing with in their life, not many would go so far as to determine why a person was constantly getting into those circumstances in the first place. This is what happened to me.

When I first went to a doctor because I suspected I had ADHD, he said I was just depressed and tried to dismiss me with a prescription for an anti-depressant. I had suffered from depression before and had been treated for it. I was sure that there was more to it than that. I wasn't getting anywhere with him. I felt belittled, patronized, and very angry. I figured there were enough doctors in town that I didn't need to waste my time with one who wasn't going to at least have an open mind. I set up an appointment with a nurse practitioner I was familiar with and she referred me to a specialist.

Never stay with a doctor who doesn't take you seriously. Many doctors don't believe that ADHD can continue into adulthood. It has always been thought of as just a childhood disease. Now that research is proving otherwise, more and more doctors are being enlightened about adult ADHD and all of the ways it can keep a person from living up to their full potential.

Women with ADHD

Women with ADHD, for the most part, appear to get very frustrated with the situations they find themselves in. They are relieved to know that there is something that can be done to help them be more productive and organized. I felt consoled knowing that my problems weren't just caused by a character flaw that I had. There was an actual physiological condition that was contributing to my erratic behavior.

A lot more is required of women now than in years past. It used to be that women could choose to stay home and focus on taking care of their family if they didn't want the added responsibility of a career. Most families now require two incomes to support them, and often in single-parent families, it is the mother who is working both jobs. Then add to it the responsibility of running a home and caring for children.

Women with ADHD find themselves often rushing and over-committing their time. They have a disorderly purse, car, closet, and household. They may go off on a tangent in a conversation, not letting anyone else get a word in. Whereas boys may be obviously hyperactive, girls tend to stay in one place and dispense excess energy with their vocal capacity.

Women typically suffer from different symptoms than those of men. This could be due to their differences in responsibilities, expectations of society, or just the basic physical differences. Here is a list of the most common symptoms that women face.

- Job Dissatisfaction
- Depression
- Feeling overwhelmed
- Chronic anxiety
- Disorganization
- Symptoms can be intensified by hormones

Men with ADHD

Most of the people I have spoken with about their experiences with ADHD are women. I have met several men who I suspect have it as well, but none of them have ever looked into the possibility. From what I have read, men don't appear to get tested as often as women do. This could be from a lack of knowledge or social stigma, or the fact that they may not think there is anything wrong with them in the first place. It is often at the request of someone else that they are finally tested.

The breakdown of a marriage, inability to hold down a job, and substance abuse all seem to be typical points at which men are confronted. They may then agree to whatever is requested of them as a last ditch effort to keep their family from falling apart. Unfortunately, until they actually believe that they have a valid issue that needs to be addressed; these attempts may be futile at best.

Society expects men to be tough. ADHD can cause a

person to be very sensitive and overly emotional. I would imagine that this can be a very difficult thing for a man to deal with. They may try to mask their feelings by going to extremes in the opposite direction. This behavior not only makes them appear to be insensitive and harsh, it can also provide a barrier that keeps others at a distance so people are less likely to challenge this handicap that only they may be aware of.

A man's self-esteem can be very fragile if they have ADHD that is not diagnosed and dealt with. The many challenges that this disorder brings along with it can cause them to fail over and over again without knowing why. If they have people depending on them, as most men do, these failures can leave them feeling disappointed in themselves. To make matters worse, the shame they feel from having disappointed those who count on them, can lead to depression as well.

Characteristics
of ADHD

Disclaimer

I in no way intend for this book to be used for self-diagnosing purposes. I am going to describe some of the traits that are most prevalent in those with ADHD. These are things that many people without ADHD may also experience, but with less severity and frequency. If you find that a majority of these characteristics pertain to you on a regular basis, you may want to seek a professional opinion. Only a doctor who is experienced with the diagnosis of the disorder is qualified to determine who has it.

Difficulty Focusing

Most people can be distracted from time to time. Those with ADHD experience this on a much larger scale that can affect their daily lives. If a person has this disorder, it does not mean they can never focus. On the contrary, sometimes they can even hyper-focus when something really interests them. Instead of attention deficit, I guess you could call it attention inconsistency. Sometimes I am so focused on something that I don't even notice what is going on around me.

Problems can arise at work or school due to directions not being followed carefully. Sometimes the ADHD person doesn't realize that they have missed vital information in a conversation until it is too late and they find themselves looking for a new job or having to retake a class when they fail. Often, when I am listening to a person talk, I will suddenly realize that I haven't been paying attention. Out of embarrassment, I tend to pretend I was listening and hope I don't look foolish later on because of it.

Reading can be difficult for me, as I'm sure it is for many with ADHD. It is not so much the reading that is the problem, as it is the comprehending of what I have read. Even without external distractions I find that I have so many things going on in my mind at the same time that I must re-read the same paragraph or page over several times before I am able to focus long enough to fully understand what I have read.

I prefer reading books that contain several short stories rather than one long novel. If the book is about something that I find very interesting, it is much easier to focus my attention. Reading assignments in school were particularly difficult for me. Even if we were given a list of books with several choices available; I typically waited until the last minute to go to the library and get it, so the best choices were already checked out by my classmates.

Focusing, or lack of focusing in this case, doesn't just

affect the momentary snippets of a person's life. While having a difficult time reading a book or holding a conversation may be frustrating, the inability to focus on one's life can be devastating. It can be nearly impossible for a person to reach their goals in life or achieve a dream that they have if they are unable to stay focused on the daily milestones that they must meet in order to make it possible.

Many times I have set a new goal for myself. Some of those times I have even gone so far as to sit down and plan out everything that I would have to do in order to accomplish that goal, and set a schedule to follow. I was still unable to obtain it. I knew exactly what I had to do, and I was fully capable of doing each step. Typically, within just a couple of days, I would have forgotten about my goal and what I was supposed to be doing. A person can do this only so many times before they get to the point where they quit setting goals in the first place. I didn't trust myself to stick with something long enough to make a difference, so why bother trying.

On a positive note, people with ADHD can be rather good at multi-tasking. Their lack of focus can make it possible for them to be working on several things at once. So long as none of these things require a lot of technical thought, a person with ADHD is able to perform like a programmed machine when doing routine tasks. Sometimes they don't even remember doing some of these things when they are done because they were busy thinking about something else at the time.

Forgetfulness

A bad memory can be a sign of ADHD. The way a doctor explained it to me is like this: having ADHD is like having a file cabinet in your brain to store all of the information, but there is no order to the filing system. All of the information may be in there, but it can't always be accessed when you need it. Sometimes you get lucky and remember it right away, and sometimes you have to keep searching through your brain for what you need.

There is a physical reason for this. The brain consists of white matter and gray matter. The gray matter is the area of the brain where information is stored: like in a computer. The white matter is a fatty substance that covers the transmitters in the brain like the rubber coating covers a printer cable. Information is sent from the gray areas throughout the brain by way of the white coated transmitters, just like information from a computer is sent to the printer through the rubber coated cable. If the rubber coating on the cable is damaged and missing in spots, the cable may short out from time to time, keeping the computer from relaying the information to the printer consistently. People with ADHD are shown to have too little white matter in their brain. This basically leaves the transmitters exposed in areas making it difficult for information to be sent to the rest of the brain consistently as well.

To make matters worse, stress can make remembering even more difficult. When you are taking a test, you may feel stressed. The stress makes it even harder to remember, which stresses you out even more. I think everyone has racked their brain from time to time, trying to remember something, only to have the answer pop into their head much later when they weren't even thinking about it.

I feel badly when someone asks me to do something for them and I forget. I've even had someone accuse me of not caring about them because I forgot to do something they had asked me to. It's not that simple. I try to write things down...then I try to remember the note.

This has even been an issue for me since being medicated for ADHD. I manage to remember most things just fine for the most part, but if something major is put on my plate that I am not used to dealing with, I tend to start forgetting some of my normal everyday tasks. It is almost as if there is a limited amount of space in my memory. If it gets too full, it starts to overflow and even things I would usually do automatically start to escape.

While this may make it sound like the medicine is not helping, it really is. To begin with, I am able to function much better on a daily basis when I am taking medicine. When I get overloaded, like I just described, it allows me to have the patience to deal with the situation in a constructive way. I may try to reassign some of my responsibilities to someone else temporarily, or just reorganize the way in which I do things so I can fit the new responsibilities in more efficiently. While I may still get frustrated with myself, I do much better at not taking it personally.

Restlessness

Everyone tends to think of ADHD as the hyperactive child who can't sit still in class. While that is one side of it, it is not always the case. I think that since it is more acceptable for boys to be hyperactive than girls, I must have found less noticeable ways to express my restlessness like jiggling my feet, tapping my pencil, and playing with my hair.

I am almost jealous of the hyperactive person who is comfortable expressing all of that energy in an external way. While their behavior may not always be socially acceptable, I know the internal stress I feel—the tenseness, eye twitching, constant worrying—is not good for my health.

Restlessness is not always visible either. I would basically describe anxiety as the hyperactivity of the brain. I have suffered from anxiety for years and it can be very frustrating. Just to sit and chit chat with someone can be difficult. There typically has to be a purpose for me to start up a conversation with someone. I can talk on the phone long enough to exchange pertinent information, but once that is covered; I find myself getting antsy and start looking for a reason to get off the phone.

This restlessness can also make it difficult to stick with one thing for any length of time. People with ADHD tend to like variety. This allows them to keep from getting bored too quickly. It could also cause them to be self-destructive in many areas of their life or they may get a reputation for not being very trustworthy.

Fortunately, I am a person who takes my responsibilities very seriously. Many times I have had that restless feeling that comes along with the powerful urge to do something drastic. It is very difficult to explain this to someone who has never experienced it before. I tend to want to run away from everything and never look back. I used to try to satisfy this urge by changing my hair color and style, or by rearranging the furniture. Sometimes this worked; sometimes it didn't, depending on my state of mind at the time. Anymore, I usually just tell myself, "this too shall pass," and I wait for the feeling to go away.

Poor Organizational Skills

People with ADHD may feel like they spend more time looking for things than anyone else. A simple project can seem much more difficult than necessary just because it would take too much time and effort to find everything needed to do the job. Things go undone because they aren't organized enough to even begin.

Poor organization can lead to poor financial management for someone with ADHD. Bills may get misplaced in all of the clutter and not get paid on time. For someone who is living paycheck to paycheck, this could result in them forgetting to set aside enough money to cover a misplaced bill, then not having anything left to pay it when it is due.

A messy and unbalanced checkbook is also a typical cause of financial problems in those with ADHD. I used to put off the annoying task of subtracting all of the checks that I had written. I thought that I was keeping track of the running balance well enough in my mind. Inevitably, I would either miscalculate my balance or forget about a check that I had written. I would then be forced to sit down and subtract it all out after receiving a statement from the bank saying that something had bounced. Once one check bounces and the fee for that is deducted, it can easily lead to more bouncing as well.

Often times, this will lead a person to go to an establishment that gives advancements on their paychecks. These places may come in handy for people who need to get their paycheck early for some reason; perhaps for extra money to take on vacation or to get something that is on sale for a limited time. Please don't ever go there to "fix" a mistake that gets you behind. Once financial mistakes lead to this option, the road back into the black can be a long and painful one.

Piles! That has got to be one of the most frustrating parts of ADHD. Things seem to accumulate everywhere. The many projects that I begin and leave lying around throughout the day can start to add up. Even if I do complete a project, most likely the items I used to complete it with will take quite some time to get back where they belong.

When it is time to sit down and eat, or watch TV, if stuff is in the way it usually just gets shifted to a pile somewhere else. Maybe it will get moved to the ironing board that didn't get folded back up. There always seems to be a favorite spot for the piles to go: a certain chair, drawer, or countertop may seem like the ideal place to put things, "just until I have time to go through them."

I have a wonderful aunt who had a very good system for her piles. When a pile got too big, or company was coming over, she would put the piles into paper bags and write the date on them. She then put the bags in her spare room. If she needed to find something, she would go to that room and find the bag with the date closest to when she last remembered seeing the item.

We didn't use the paper bag system, but we did have one of those "spare rooms" when I was growing up. We called it the elephant room, because you could have hid an elephant in there for all of the stuff. I guess it is not surprising that our family never had guests actually stay in the spare room. That could have been disastrous. As I am writing this, I am left wondering how much of the ADHD behavior is symptomatic and how much is just learned from our relatives! That could be a whole other book.

Impulsivity

Those with ADHD can be very impulsive. I frequently find myself getting into messes because I tend to act first and think later. I say things without properly phrasing my thoughts and it comes out all wrong or I say things when I should have kept my mouth shut altogether. I like to think that I have gotten better at this over the years, but I'm not always so sure.

When I was taking a Group Dynamics class in college in 1984, the class was divided up into groups for different projects and experiments. I was in a group that was observed through a two-way mirror. We were just told to have a conversation, and were given a topic to discuss. Then, each person in another group was assigned a person in our group to observe. Each time "their person" interrupted another member of the group, it was to be noted. Afterward, when the real reason for our discussion was announced, we were told how many times we had interrupted someone else in our group. I was shocked at the results. I was told that I had interrupted the other members of my group over twenty times during the ten minute discussion. Everyone else in the group had less than five interruptions. Some didn't have any. I had no idea that I even did this, let alone did it so often. I have tried to make a conscious effort not to since. This can be difficult for me though, because usually when I stop myself and wait for the other person to finish; I end up forgetting what I was going to say.

After learning that interrupting is a common side effect of having ADHD, I started paying closer attention to it in conversations and making note of those who do it often. It can be rather comical to watch a conversation between several people who all have ADHD. I have done this a couple of times with my two ADHD positive children and my mom, who I am sure has it too. It is as if we are having four separate conversations at the same time. Nobody is allowed to get a full thought out before someone else breaks in.

Standing in line, or waiting for something, may seem unbearable to a person who is impulsive. I have damaged many items while removing them from their packaging because I couldn't wait to get the proper tool to open it. It seems funny to admit this now, because when my daughter was a child, I would get so upset with her for doing the same thing. Sometimes packages would get so damaged or were thrown away without looking at them, that the directions are unreadable or lost. That can be a problem … if you bother to read the directions in the first place. I am embarrassed to admit that I am a life-long member of the "If at first it doesn't work, read the directions" club. I always think it will be so much faster to figure things out myself. Unfortunately, this rarely works.

Impulsive behavior can cause minor annoyances such as these, but there are far greater difficulties that people get into because of sudden impulses they seem incapable of controlling: unplanned pregnancy, sexually transmitted diseases, and car accidents for example. My son with ADHD was once hit by a gas truck while he was riding his snowmobile. He drove right out into the roadway without looking. Luckily, he acted quickly enough and was able to swing the back end of this sled around before the truck hit him. He was pushed down the icy road rather than run over. Unfortunately, the truck ended up in the ditch because of his actions.

Once I rode my bike out into the road right in front of a car when I was young. I hadn't even realized that I had done it until the people came back to yell at me. Another time I came less than an inch away from losing an eye when I was hit in the face by the corner of a sharp metal swing. I was running around the yard yelling, "The fruit man's here, the fruit man's here!" and of course, not watching where I was going, I ran right in front of my brother as he was swinging. Apparently, I got really excited about fruit when I was a child. Fortunately, for today's ADHD children, they don't make those sharp cornered metal swings anymore. For that matter, I don't think anyone delivers fruit door to door anymore either.

Creativity

One of those good things about ADHD that I mentioned in the introduction is the abundance of creativity that tends to come with the presence of ADHD. I am a person who likes to know why things happen. Why, for example, does a person with ADHD have so many deficiencies, while they appear to have such an abundance of creativity? I had to figure this out for myself, so I went to Wikipedia, an online encyclopedia, for some answers. Although they didn't come right out and answer this question, per se, I was able to dig out enough scientific information to come to my own conclusion about this matter.

I began by looking into dopamine. Dopamine is a neurotransmitter that is produced in the brain. It is then transported to different parts of the brain by way of four major pathways. A deficient amount of dopamine in the frontal lobe is said to cause impulsivity, inattentiveness, and a lack of problem solving abilities. This deficiency is thought to be associated with ADHD. Dopamine reaches this area by way of the Mesolimbic Pathway, which branches off, sending dopamine first to a few other areas of the brain before reaching the frontal lobe, the pathway's furthest and final destination.

If the frontal lobe is not getting enough dopamine, I would then assume that as long as the dopamine is reaching the other parts of the brain, that the Mesolimbic Pathway services, it must be getting backed up in the pathway somewhere. Imagine an irrigation hose that is running uphill. If it is working properly, the water will be moving at a steady pace while being distributed evenly to all of the areas on the hillside as well as the plants on top of the hill. If the faucet is turned down slightly, reducing the power behind the flow, the water may reach the areas on the side of the hill, but only provide an occasional drop of water to the plants on top. The water would be backed up in the hose.

I admit that I don't have a degree in science, but I do like to think that I have some common sense. When I read about the effect that dopamine has on creativity, it all started to come together. Apparently, when dopamine is backed up in the Mesolimbic Pathway, it increases the creative drive. This is exactly what I was looking for. The circumstances that occur in the brain which cause the deficiencies of ADHD are directly linked to the circumstances that increase the creative drive.

I have often wondered, as I'm sure many have, if having ADHD results in a person exhibiting more creative tendencies, will medicating that person to control their ADHD behavior diminish the enhanced creativity as well? If the conclusion that I have come to is correct, I would think that medication would indeed affect creativity; since basically the job of a stimulant is to help push the dopamine up into the frontal lobe, or turn the faucet up so to speak, it would then remove the cause of the increased creative drive. Again, this is just my own theory. I have never been able to find any definite information on this topic as of yet, so I have used my own research to come to this conclusion.

I have had creative tendencies for as long as I can remember. It is almost like an uncontrollable force that causes me to want to make things, improve things, or express myself in some obnoxious way. Along with this exuding craftiness, I also have the problem of getting frustrated when I reach uncharted territory. If I get to a point where I'm not sure what to do next, I tend to put everything away until later. Many times, later never comes.

This book, for example, spent about five years getting shifted from one computer to another. I hate to think about how many times I considered deleting it altogether. I didn't know how to get it published. Everywhere I looked online for advice on the subject I was only left with more questions. It wasn't until I had been on medication for quite some time that I was finally able to find an avenue for my work. Medication, while it may take away the increased creative drive, doesn't take away creativity altogether. What good is creativity anyway if it doesn't get put to good use?

The disorganization and lack of direction that always seems to be present can frustrate a person to the point of giving up. If the creativity that comes out of having ADHD is properly channeled, wonderful things can happen. It is very important to be surrounded by encouraging people. When those with ADHD find themselves at a dead end and consider throwing in the towel on an important project, these people can help them keep their ideas heading in the right direction.

As great as creativity can be, it could also be another way that a person with ADHD gets behind schedule. The drive to do everything in a different and creative way could make things take longer than necessary. This could cause something to not get done on time, or not get done at all.

An example of this could be when a person with ADHD has the small task of filing a few papers. They may decide to set up a whole new and improved filing system while they're at it. This then results in them having to take out all of the files and start fresh. A job that should have only taken a couple of minutes may take hours. They may run out of steam or time halfway through the project and end up with more files being left out than they had to put away to begin with.

Another example may be when a cook with ADHD, instead of simply making sandwiches like they were instructed to do, suddenly feels compelled to put cute little smiley faces on each one. Rather than hearing the excited oohs and awws of the people as they receive their sandwiches, the cook may very well hear the grumbling over another late meal instead.

Author's Clarification

The rest of the characteristics I am going to discuss are different from the ones that were just covered. Whereas the previous characteristics are symptoms of having ADHD, the ones I am about to explain are caused by having to deal with the symptoms of ADHD. I know this sounds very confusing, so I will clarify my theory further.

Difficulty focusing, forgetfulness, restlessness, poor organizational skills, impulsivity, and creativity are all caused by the actual physiological differences in the brain of a person with ADHD. The next characteristics I am going to describe: inability to complete tasks, relationship difficulties, substance abuse, depression, frequent job changes, and frequent change of residence, are not so much caused by having ADHD, as they are caused by being impulsive, restless, forgetful, etc., which just happen to be the physiological symptoms of ADHD.

There are three basis kinds of ADHD: inattentive, impulsive, and combined. A person who has been diagnosed with this disorder will have some or all the symptoms I have just mentioned. Which symptoms they have will depend on which type of ADHD they have. From my research of the brain, I am led to believe that the inattentiveness is caused by the deficiency of white matter, the impulsive is caused by the deficiency of dopamine in the frontal lobe, and the combined is caused by problems in both areas of the brain.

I should also add, that while these next characteristics are all common among those with ADHD, I believe that a person's self-esteem, emotional support system, and resources all play an important role in whether or not they become an issue. From my experience, it appears as if those with close knit families and higher income tend to be effected by ADHD in less traumatic ways. They have the financial stability and emotional support already in place. Since having ADHD can make it difficult for a person to hold down a job and create stable relationships, those without these advantages to begin with are more likely to suffer from the characteristics I am about to describe.

Inability to Complete Tasks

Difficulty focusing can make completing tasks more challenging for those with ADHD. They may not be able to finish because they are so distracted by what is going on around them, or because they have too much going on in their head. This can be particularly difficult if there is a time schedule to stick to. The added stress might cause them to make unnecessary mistakes because they find themselves rushing under the pressure. If the task is new to the individual, the focusing difficulty may begin with the frustration of simply not being able to understand the directions. The task itself may not even get started, let alone completed.

Organizational skills are also important when completing tasks. I am far less likely to start a project if I can't find the items I need to complete it. Remember the piles I mentioned? Even if I do manage to find what I am looking for, chances are, it will take so long that I won't have the time or desire to complete the task anyway.

Many times I have offered to help my mom with projects. Typically, this begins with us searching for whatever necessary items we might need, which results in us finding some really fun things that we haven't seen in awhile. We usually end up reminiscing and having lots of fun, but rarely accomplish what we started out to do. Sometimes we try to accomplish way more than time will allow and the project is left half done.

Occasionally, I will go to her house to do the project when she is not at home. I will either bring what I need to do the job, or have her find it and set it out for me before she leaves. I manage to get a lot more done this way. It's not nearly as much fun, but way more productive.

Relationship Difficulties

Poor impulse control can lead someone to be overly sensitive to what others say or do, causing them to withdraw and avoid people. At the other end of the spectrum, it could make them lash out at others. Those with ADHD tend to be quick to react, but they can be quick to calm down and forget about it too. Either way, this poor impulse control can make it difficult for them to create and maintain healthy relationships.

By being overly sensitive, their partner may find it impossible to maintain honest communication with them for fear of hurting their feelings. In another situation, extreme sensitivity could leave a person vulnerable to a partner who is controlling and overbearing. If a person's poor impulse control is exhibited by being hurtful and insensitive toward their partner, they may spout off the nasty comments in their head without thinking about the consequences until it is too late.

Poor socialization skills are common in people with ADHD. They may have a difficult time refraining from saying exactly what they think when they think it, no matter how inappropriate it may be. Social cues tend to slip past them somehow as well. Whereas most people, when in an unfamiliar social situation, tend to look for the subtle gestures of those around them as a guide for proper behavior, the poor impulse control and inattentiveness of ADHD can make this nearly impossible. They may focus only on what they see right in front of them as everything else goes unnoticed.

Typically, people learn how to interact with others at a very young age. I remember having a difficult time making friends when I was a child. I was shy and very self-conscious until I got to know someone. Once I felt comfortable with them, I couldn't seem to shut myself up. Even once I realized that people could get upset by things that I said, I had a difficult time controlling myself. I may have tried to hold back by telling myself, "don't say it," just to have the words come flying out of my mouth anyway.

I knew I was different from other kids at school. I'm not sure if it helped or hurt that I attended a very small school. If I had attended a large school as my children did, I believe there would have been substantially more kids like me who didn't fit in as well. In some magical way, when enough misfits get together, they aren't misfits anymore. They just become one of the many cliques.

I led a pretty sheltered childhood for the most part, but I was in a lot of different 4-H groups. When I was fourteen, I was a counselor for a 4-H youth camp. I was with people I had never met before. Most importantly, they had never met me. I had only ever been around the same kids in my small town and they knew all of my idiosyncrasies. I now had an opportunity to start fresh with a whole new group of people.

I managed to keep in touch with several of the other counselors for quite awhile through letter writing, but the one who made the biggest difference in my life was a fourteen-year-old boy from a neighboring community. He wasn't actually even involved in camp. His best friend was a counselor and his little brother was one of the camp kids. His name was Tim, and he changed my life.

Now, you may be expecting a story of young love and all the gooey stuff that goes along with it, but that's not the way it was. Tim was everybody's friend. He accepted people for who they were and encouraged them to be just that and nothing more. I had never experienced this kind of acceptance from a peer with so many other friends before. Typically, I was the last friend that a peer would choose to spend time with if they had other options. If he was hanging out with other friends and I showed up, he would ask me to tag along too. I suddenly had more friends than I had ever had before.

The funny thing is, by being accepted for who I was, I found I changed. I felt better about myself and I took pride in my appearance. This allowed me to accomplish more things; things that I might otherwise not have had the courage to do. I became more outgoing and started taking leadership positions that became available to me.

I went to Washington D.C. to represent my county, I became a 4-H leader to teach young girls how to sew, and I attended leadership conferences, just to name a few. I felt like I had a voice people wanted to listen to for the first time.

When I am taking a prescription for ADHD, I usually do okay when interacting with people on a daily basis. I can do what I need to do and things go smoothly for the most part. If I am under a lot of additional stress and my schedule gets overbooked, I may find myself falling back into some of the old ADHD ways. Even though I am still taking medicine, I have a hard time focusing on what people are saying because I have too much on my mind, or I will start getting unorganized again and forget to do everything I need to do.

When this happens, I make concessions for myself, because I realize how bad it could be. Although I may not be performing at my best, at least I am not performing at my worst. Several years ago, after losing my insurance and having to stop taking my medication, I found myself under a great deal of stress. I verbally lashed out at people to a point where I was unrecognizable to myself and others who knew me.

The first time this happened was when I lost my temper with a cashier at a local store. I'm not even sure why I got upset with her anymore, but I remember there were a lot of witnesses. Worst of all, my thirteen-year-old daughter was with me at the time. As soon as we walked out of the store, she looked at me and said, "Who are you, and what did you do with my mother?" I felt so bad for the way I had behaved that I couldn't even bring myself to go back into that store for a very long time. When I did return, I felt so ashamed, I avoided her line.

Nearly a year later, I decided I had to apologize to her or I would never be able to get past this. I approached her and described the scene that I had caused and how badly I felt. She said she had no idea what I was talking about, but I had made her day. Apparently, people were always being rude to her, but she had never had a single person come back to apologize before. So, in the end, she was happy and I could hold my head up when I walked through the store again. I can count these outbursts I have had on one hand, but that is still too many times in my opinion.

Somewhere along the line, I feel like I missed the secret code for juggling friends. I now refrain from having too many close friends at once. I can have one at a time, but add a few more and I end up feeling like one or more is always mad at me. I may have inadvertently broken one friend's confidence by telling another something I shouldn't have, or invited one to do something and made another feel left out. I should be very sore from all of the times I have kicked myself over the years for things I have said or done without thinking first.

Years ago, unintentionally really, I started cutting ties with people. I got so frustrated with myself and the situations I kept finding myself in that it was easier to just avoid everyone. Some people, I had a feeling I had done something to upset them, but didn't know what I had done. Others, I just didn't see for long periods of time and didn't want to have to re-cap the details of my life. It was bad enough having to live it without having to give someone a play-by-play as well.

Substance Abuse

The most commonly abused substances are drugs, alcohol, caffeine, and food, but some other things that people use to the point of abuse are sex/pornography, gambling, and thrill-seeking activities such as bungee jumping, car racing, and sky diving. These things can get out of control for the average person, but when you're dealing with someone who already has issues with control, they can be devastating.

When people are left undiagnosed or decide not to take medication, they may turn to stimulants to feel more "normal." This may include using nicotine, amphetamines, or caffeine. Since most medications for ADHD are stimulants, this makes sense. Some people turn to other substances such as alcohol or marijuana, which aren't stimulants, but help to numb the feelings of frustration or poor self-esteem. The major problem with doing this is that when they sober up, the problems haven't gone away. Most likely, they have even made them worse with their choice of "self-medication."

I believe the choices a person makes, whether they have ADHD or not, depend on how they were raised, the examples they had set for them, and the things they have experienced in life. We look at our surroundings and experiences as we are growing up, and use those examples to guide us. Unfortunately, those with ADHD were often times raised by a person or persons who also have ADHD. The example someone best relates to may not necessarily be their parents either. Sometimes parents may set good examples, but their child may be more impressed by the actions of someone else in their life instead. The important thing to remember is that once a person learns what is right, regardless of how they were raised, it is ultimately their responsibility to try and make good and healthy decisions.

Most people will naturally turn to what they are familiar with. If they grew up around alcohol, this may be the first place they look for comfort. How they handle it will most likely be determined by the examples in their life. Some people may do their drinking at the bar where they can unload to whoever plops down on the bar stool next to them. Others may try to hide the fact that they are drinking. They and everyone else around them pretend it doesn't exist and everything is just fine. While this is one more example of an elephant in the room often associated with ADHD, alcoholism is by no means exclusive to those with ADHD. I should also clarify here that the art of trying to appear as if nothing is wrong has been practiced by mankind since Adam and Eve. It is typically resorted to when people are embarrassed or unsure how to respond to a situation. ADHD holds no patent on this behavior as well.

Sometimes addictions begin when a person finds something that fills a void in their life. When I was about fifteen and started making new friends and becoming more confident, not all of the changes I made were for the good. I started getting attention from boys for the first time in my life, and I didn't quite know how to handle this. I have tried many times to figure out why I got such a high every time a guy showed an interest in me. Perhaps the years of feeling self-conscious and awkward around my peers are what primed me for this addiction. Maybe it was the feeling I had that my father didn't think I was good enough that made the affection of the opposite sex so appealing. I will probably never know for sure, but whatever it was, my impulsive ADHD nature made it very difficult for me to resist the advances that I was starting to receive. Luckily, the fear I had that my father would kill me if I got pregnant kept me from losing my virginity for a very long time. For the most part, a heated kiss was enough for me to get a "fix."

I wish I had had more self-control back then. It was a constant battle between the angel and devil sitting on my shoulder—between feeling accepted by others and feeling acceptable to myself. Everyone needs to realize that they have choices. There is a saying that a person needs to hit rock bottom before they can come back up. That isn't necessarily true. Once a person realizes they are heading in the wrong direction, they can turn back at any time. It won't be easy and it may take several tries to finally succeed. The key is that they recognize it and are determined to keep trying for as long as it takes.

Depression

One of the symptoms a person with ADHD may have is depression. They may suffer from poor self-esteem when they can't figure out why they have such a hard time succeeding in life. Once diagnoses are complete, through treatment and understanding of the defect, a person will hopefully learn to be less harsh on themselves and the feelings of depression will subside.

This can be much harder than expected though. To begin with, the depression may not be that directly linked to the ADHD and may be a condition in itself that could make the ADHD harder to treat. The depression might have to be controlled before the ADHD treatment can be successful, or the doctor may choose to treat both simultaneously.

I suffered with depression for years. When I learned that I had ADHD and was going through life feeling like a loser and a quitter because of this genetic, physiological disorder, I did feel a sense of relief in knowing that I had been at an unfair disadvantage. The depression didn't go away completely, but I did allow myself some concessions when things didn't turn out the way I had hoped. It took quite some time to get to the point where I could recognize when my ADHD was getting the best of me. I now know when I need to have my medication adjusted and when I need to adjust the way I am dealing with a situation. This does not mean that I always follow my instincts though. Knowing what you need to do and doing it are two completely different things.

Everyone is different and will have their own issues that they bring to the table. That is why it is so important to have someone to confide in. A support system is the key to a person's mental health. Depression can cause someone to go into a shell and not participate in life at all, or it could cause them to take it out on those around them and become verbally or physically abusive. Sometimes a person's depression can go undetected for years until one day they take their own life and their loved ones are left wondering why they didn't see any signs. Please, talk to someone about it if you are feeling depressed or may be thinking about suicide. If you have a friend or family member you can confide in, tell them. They can help you set up an appointment with your doctor who can then see that you get the help you need. They may even be willing to go with you to your appointment. Check your local yellow pages for emergency hotlines run by mental health centers or hospitals. They will be able to direct you to resources in your area. Keep the number handy if you need someone to talk to. If you are feeling desperate and time is of the essence, go to the nearest emergency room immediately.

The disasters we seem to bring upon ourselves when we suffer from ADHD can feel like such a heavy load. When undiagnosed, a person doesn't understand why they continue to find themselves in the same dark hole over and over again. Once a person learns that they have ADHD and understand why they do these self-destructive things, without some kind of treatment, they may still not be able to change that behavior. To make matters worse, the oversensitivity and impulsiveness that accompany ADHD may make it difficult for a person with depression to deal with it in a constructive way. They may have an overwhelming feeling of helplessness and impending doom.

When my second marriage fell apart, I still had not been diagnosed. I became so depressed that I could hardly get out of bed in the morning. The responsibility of having to take care of my children is all that kept me going at times. I tried my best to hide my frustration from them by putting on a happy face. I felt strongly that since my children were not in any way responsible for what I had gotten myself into, it should not be taken out on them. After all, I was the one who jumped into another hasty marriage brought on by another unplanned pregnancy and was once again losing my home and family. This time though, I was coming out of it with two more children to think of.

Due to my change in employment, I could only afford a one bedroom apartment. Shortly after I left my husband, I quit my job as a private duty home health aid, and I took a job working as a cashier at a convenience store. The money I made didn't cover all of my bills and I found myself drowning in debt to the point where I was not going to be able to pay my rent. I was also receiving harassing phone calls from the credit card company and getting disconnection notices in the mail. I felt I couldn't do anything right and that my children would truly be better off without me.

I didn't want to leave my children with the legacy of having a mother who committed suicide, so when I heard of some teens who died accidentally, I decided to set up the exact scenario for myself to make my suicide look like an accident. I would rather not elaborate on the steps that I took to accomplish this. If a reader is considering suicide but doesn't for the same reason I hesitated, I don't want to give them any ideas. Fortunately, my attempt didn't work. I don't know what I did or didn't do that changed the outcome, but I am so glad today that I got it wrong. I like to think that I got it right. I guess God still had plans for me.

After that, the seriousness of my actions started to weigh on me and I finally confided in a friend. She made me tell my soon-to-be ex-husband what I had done. She said that if I didn't tell him, she would. I thought it would be better coming from me, so I told him. He took me to the hospital to get the help that I needed.

While being in the hospital for a week gave me a chance to get away from my problems for awhile and start taking medication to help with my depression; I was now left with the stigma of having been in a psychiatric unit. I tried to comfort myself with the fact that there was even a police officer in there with me (and no, he was not on duty ... he was another patient). It wasn't a bunch of "crazy people" screaming and running around. They were just normal, everyday people who had reached their breaking point and needed a break because of it.

When I left the hospital, I didn't have any place to go. Since the divorce wasn't final yet, I moved into the third floor of our home. It made sense to do this since our two kids already had bedrooms on the second floor with their dad. I thought this would be the best way for the kids to get to spend time with me and their older brother until I was able to get into the low income townhouse I had applied for. I tried to stay out of sight as much as possible when the kid's father was home, but tensions still ran high. One evening, he came up to the third floor while I was watching television and sat down. He started taking out his frustration on me: saying what he thought of me and my inability to get my life straightened out. I don't remember any of his exact words. I just remember coming out of that lecture feeling like a lousy mother, and there was no point in even going on. It was hard to believe that this was the same guy who just a few weeks earlier had tearfully left me in a hospital room so I wouldn't kill myself. Now, he was the one making me feel that way all over again.

I left the house and drove to the store. I bought some stationary, alcohol, and a couple of boxes of sleeping pills. I wasn't worried about my suicide being known anymore. After what I had just been told, I thought my kids would be so much happier and more secure without me around that it didn't really matter. I drove to a local park and started drinking. As I drank I began writing letters to the people in my life. I wrote one to each of my children. I tried to explain to them how much I loved them and that they would be so much better off without me messing up their lives.

I saved the hardest letter for last. As I was writing to my mother, I couldn't help but think how this would affect her. Of all the things I feared in the world, the thing I feared most was the thought of losing one of my children. They meant more to me than anything else in the world. I couldn't bring that kind of pain to my mom. I returned to the third floor of the house and pulled myself up by my boot straps.

I wish I could say that this was the last time the idea of suicide became a possibility for me, but I can't. There was one more time that I came to that painful point in my life. I had already been diagnosed with ADHD and had taken medication for some time. Due to a change in the insurance that I received through my employer, my prescriptions were no longer covered with a small co-pay. I was now required to pay a percentage of the cost. Prescriptions for ADHD can be very expensive, so even that percentage was more than I could afford to pay. I had to stop taking my medication.

Shortly after this, an old boyfriend who I hadn't heard from in years contacted me. I very quickly jumped into a relationship with him. I hadn't taken the time necessary to see that after over twenty years, the behavior that caused me to break up with him in high school was still very much a part of who he was. Even though I wasn't pregnant, and I hadn't rushed into a marriage with him, he and I both had children involved and they had gotten attached to each other. All of them except for my middle child; he moved in with his father and step-mother. My years of unpredictable behavior were starting to get to him. I also had a lot of respect for this man's parents. I knew if I broke his heart again, they would never forgive me.

I decided that I had gotten myself into this mess, and I was just going to have to live with it. Why should so many people have to suffer because of my stupid, impulsive behavior? Not to mention how badly I knew I would feel about hurting him and his family again. The relationship continued out of guilt, but eventually I got to a point where I just couldn't keep up the charade any longer.

I came up with another "accidental" way to end my life. I decided to do it on an evening when the kids would be with their father. I had it all planned out, and on the day of its execution, God called in a stay. That morning, I went to church with my mom for what I thought would be the last time. As I was sitting there in the pew waiting for the service to start, I began to pray. If God was real, like I had been taught all through my life, I wanted him to send me a sign during the service. If he didn't want me to take my own life, I wanted him to tell me what to do instead. As much as I begged for him to do this, I was really just expecting for the message that morning to be inspiring and pertinent to my situation. What I learned instead was that when God wants to send a message, he doesn't mess around.

The youth and family pastor began to speak that morning. He suddenly stopped talking and paused for a moment. He said that he couldn't continue just yet because he believed that he had a message from God for someone in the congregation. I don't think he had ever done anything quite like this before and he seemed almost unsure about whether or not he should have spoken up. He continued by saying, "God wants you to tell someone." He then read a verse from the Bible about how a rope on its own may not be very strong, but when two or more are woven together, they can bear a much heavier load. He then continued with his regular service.

I hadn't told anyone what I was planning to do. I felt so badly for what I had put my family and friends through the first time I attempted suicide that I didn't want them to know that I was feeling that way again. After the service, I still didn't tell anyone for quite some time. I didn't feel the need to anymore. God had sent me a personal message! With Him on my side, I knew I would be able to handle any situation I got myself into.

It is hard for people to understand just how overwhelming little things can appear to someone with ADHD who suffers from depression. Looking back on it now, from a medicated stand point, it all seems pretty silly. I should have just ended the relationship and got on with my life. It's not like we were even living together. It shouldn't have been so difficult. As simple as that sounds to me now, without being on my medication, I felt overwhelmed and unable to cope with the thought of hurting someone and having them all hate me.

If a person who has ADHD knows that they are genetically predisposed to depression or if they are having suicidal thoughts, it is even more important for them to find someone to confide in. Hopefully, with support and the proper medication, they will be strong enough to handle difficult times so they don't do something that will undoubtedly change the lives of everyone who loves them.

Frequent Job Changes

Not everyone who has ADHD changes jobs frequently. Some people I suspect to have ADHD have been at the same job for many years. For example, a post hole digger with ADHD may be very content with their job. It doesn't require a lot of social contact, confusing directions, or opportunity for failure. If there is no real reason to change, it makes sense to stay at the same job. On the other hand, if they really dislike their job or if the pay is not enough for them to get by, a person with ADHD may avoid looking for a different job for the wrong reason. Perhaps they are frustrated by having to fill out all of the job applications. Maybe it has been so long since they have had to look for another job that they aren't sure where to begin. Some people find a certain comfort in doing the same job every day and don't want to lose that security, even if it isn't the best thing for them.

Many people with ADHD change jobs frequently due to being fired. They may find it difficult to get to work on time, or even remember their schedule. Some are fired because they fail to learn what is necessary to do the job right, or because of their inability to get along with coworkers.

Still another group of ADHD'ers change jobs frequently for a reason that many are not aware of. There is a restless feeling that keeps them looking for a career that will be more satisfying. The problem with this is that no job ever seems to meet this requirement forever. After a couple of years, these people usually feel like they have gotten about as much as they can get out of a job and start to look for another.

This could be brought on simply because of their need for variety and an outlet for their creativity. Not many jobs meet these criteria. Typically, these jobs come in the form of careers that require a college education. Many with ADHD have a difficult time finding the funding for college, let alone making it through years of schooling. The creative satisfaction they may have been able to get in a field such as engineering, graphic design, or advertising may be hard for them to come by otherwise.

Some people with ADHD may dread going to work simply because they are so overwhelmed with everything they need to do in their life. This dread may be misinterpreted as dissatisfaction with their job, when in all reality, once they get to work, they end up enjoying themselves. I think this last one best describes me. Being an Activities Director at an assisted living community provides me with the flexibility, creativity, variety, and fun that keep me loving my job. The problem is, as much as I enjoy it, I don't want to go to work. I always feel so far behind in everything at home that I don't feel like I have time for it. Once I get to work, I find my job to be very satisfying.

I think this also has a lot to do with my age. I was raised during a time when women could decide if they wanted to work outside of the home or not. When I was growing up, I wanted to be a housewife and mother. I would take care of my life-size baby doll and dream of having kids some day. I had no plans of going to college. I didn't want a career. I just wanted to take care of my home and family. By working full-time, no matter how rewarding my job may be, I am not left with enough time to take care of my home or family in the manner that I would like to.

While I am positive that this scenario is not exclusive to women with ADHD, I believe this disorder has caused me to leave perfectly satisfying jobs due to a restlessness and impulsiveness that I did not recognize at the time. Now that I have figured out the cause of my reluctance to go to work, I can simply accept it as something that I have to do and just be happy that at least I have an enjoyable job to go to.

Frequent Change of Residence

People with ADHD may have a hard time planting themselves in one location. Whether they move often because they are restless, or simply because their unpredictable financial status makes it difficult for them to maintain the same living conditions, the end result remains the same. Moving frequently may make it very difficult for them and their family to put down the solid foundation necessary for a successful future.

After my second divorce, I moved approximately twenty times in six years. Fortunately, most of the locations were within a few miles of each other. Usually, when I moved, it was because I thought it would make things much better. One of those times was when I moved back in with by ex-husband, who assured me things would be different. When things weren't different, I had to move again. Of course, the move out of my ex's house was quick, impulsive, and unplanned; so I took whatever accommodations I could find in a pinch. Once I found a more appropriate place for the kids and myself, I would move again. That one, emotional, poor decision to try and get the family back together ended up adding another three moves to my history.

My moves typically occurred because I had big plans and dreams. I would then have to move again when my big plans and dreams failed to materialize. I felt so badly for uprooting my children over and over again that I got to where I could move everything we had during a weekend that the kids were with their father. I would get as much put away as possible before they returned so it would feel like home to them.

Seeking a Diagnosis

Find a Support System

If you have read to this point and think you may have ADHD, you might be ready to seek a diagnosis from a specialist. The process may not be as easy as you think. Before you begin, it would be a good idea to find a support system. I have a very hard time with follow through. When the going gets tough, I just want to go to sleep and try to forget about it. I don't recommend that. It helps to tell someone who cares about you what you are doing. Make sure it is someone who is supportive of your decision and will encourage you to keep going in the diagnostic process when you get frustrated.

It may be difficult to find a doctor who will take this seriously, but you will need a doctor to refer you to a specialist. Adult ADHD is a new enough discovery that there are even doctors who will discourage you from being tested. Or, if they don't actually discourage you, they won't be of any help. My first doctor was like that.

I got the feeling that he thought I was just seeking controlled prescription drugs. There are plenty of doctors out there, so you don't need to waste your time talking to one who doesn't take you seriously.

Look Into Your History

Since ADHD hasn't been treated for very long, you may have a hard time finding people in your family tree who have been diagnosed with it, especially adults. Make a list of those in your family who have been diagnosed, both older and younger than you, and their relationship to you. Those who haven't been diagnosed, but most likely have ADHD, can also be added to the list. You can use the characteristics of ADHD and attempt to identify family members who have a lot of the qualities an ADHD person would have.

It isn't very difficult to determine which adults have struggled with the disorder. Adults with ADHD tend to be at a poorer economic status than the rest of their siblings, as well as being in a lower position on the society totem pole. They are also the family members associated with frequent divorce, job changes, and changes of residence, multiple car accidents, learning disabilities, emotional disorders, and substance abuse. If you are unsure if you have ADHD in your family tree, think about those relatives closest to you and see if any of them show a lot of these signs. Once you have thought of some, use the list of characteristics in this book to further narrow down the possibility. It is not necessary to go to these family members to tell them of your suspicions. Some people may get very upset at the insinuation. If you decide to go in for a diagnosis, you just need a general idea, not documented cases, of whether others in your family history have it as well. If you do have ADHD, most likely the list will be very long.

Your personal history will be an important factor in diagnosing whether you have ADHD or not. Impulse control issues, poor judgment, and not paying attention when you were a child could possibly be identified by writing down injuries you sustained when young. These would be injuries sustained while not watching where you were going, doing dangerous things repeatedly, or because you couldn't wait until the time was right to do something.

In order for a formal diagnosis to be made, you must have signs that go back to your early childhood years, before the age of seven. ADHD always starts out as a childhood disease. Sometimes those signs may not be very noticeable, or you may not remember them personally. Talk to parents, siblings, and other people who knew you as a child for help with this. The thing about me that stood out most was how impulsive I was. I may not have remembered this had I not been injured so many times because of it. If you cannot find any early signs of ADHD, a positive diagnosis will most likely not be made. Instead, you might want to think back to head injuries or a trauma which took place shortly before the first signs began.

It helps to ask a parent or a teacher you had as a child about your behavior in school. Most children with ADHD may not think they are a handful, but I'm sure the adults responsible for them would see things differently. Try to find old report cards. Look for teacher comments such as "doesn't use time wisely" or "not using full potential." I took my mom with me when I was tested for ADHD at the age of thirty-six. It had been quite some time since I was a child and it helped for the doctor to be able to talk to her personally. He asked questions that resulted in her remembering things about me as a child that we had not considered to be a potential sign of ADHD.

Testing

Try to get a good night's sleep before your test. It is an all day event. I had a very lengthy questionnaire to fill out, as well as being asked several questions by the doctor. There were a series of verbal tests, as well as some done on the computer.

Unfortunately, there isn't a blood test that can be done to give a definitive diagnosis. This causes many to be skeptical about the existence of the disorder at all. Studies are still being done to try and find the gene for ADHD, and scientists have been attempting to use brain scans to search for a consistent link between those positively diagnosed. With continued studies in this area, perhaps a simple medical test will be all that is needed for diagnosis someday.

After Diagnosis

Treatment

Once a formal diagnosis has been made, the test results will be sent to your regular doctor. You should set up an appointment with them to discuss how you want to treat it. While the symptoms of ADHD may be somewhat consistent from person to person, how interruptive it is in their lives can vary. Some people may find ADHD to be merely an inconvenience, while others see it as being debilitating. It should be treated accordingly.

Medication may not be for everyone. I personally don't like to be without it if I have to be productive or sociable. I keep my pills by my bed, so I can take it immediately upon waking. After about a half hour, I feel focused and optimistic. I can't wait to get out of bed and start getting things done.

Medications for ADHD can be very expensive. Some insurance companies in the past have not recognized Adult ADHD and did not cover prescriptions for it. I became aware of that nine years ago when I was diagnosed. Hopefully, this is not the case anymore. A majority of the most widely used ADHD medications now have generic forms that are more affordable. This makes for lower co-pays when you have insurance coverage, but it can still be very costly if you have to purchase it yourself. Your doctor may be able to provide samples for you to get started. This could allow you to find one that works best for you without a large initial investment. Some pharmaceutical companies will help low income patients by providing prescriptions as well.

Certain individuals benefit greatly from seeing a psychiatrist or counselor. This can be particularly beneficial if you have some of the associated co-morbid disorders as well. Make sure your insurance will cover these visits before scheduling them. If it is not covered, there may be agencies available that provide services on a sliding fee scale so you only pay what you can afford to.

I am writing this with the assumption that my readers may be at a disadvantage financially. I realize this may not be the case. For those who are lucky enough to not have to worry about the cost of their treatment, you can skip this section and go on to the next. I would like to cover this topic a little further though, as my experiences with medical coverage have been a little unpredictable from time to time.

My medical coverage has taken many forms over the course of treating my ADHD. I have gone through periods where I have been covered under someone else's insurance, I have had my own insurance, I have used Medicaid, and at times I was left uninsured. I noticed a pattern starting to form when I was covered by Medicaid.

It was while I had Medicaid coverage that I was diagnosed with ADHD and I found a medication that worked for me. After being treated for awhile, I began to be more successful in my work, was better at budgeting, and started making better decisions in general. I felt much better about myself. I reached the point where I was making too much money to qualify for Medicaid and my coverage was dropped. Without coverage, I couldn't afford my prescriptions. Once off of my medication, I started having a hard time functioning again. I couldn't keep track of my finances, wasn't working as much, and became very depressed again. I ended up back on Medicaid and could resume taking my medicine. The prescription made an immediate difference and I began focusing on getting myself back on track only to have the same thing happen again.

If you find yourself in this scenario, I would highly recommend that you make it a priority to find a job with medical insurance while you are on your medication and doing well. The constant yo-yoing on and off medication is not good for a person, and the ups and downs financially can be emotionally draining as well. If you find a job with insurance coverage and are able to stay on your medication consistently, you are more likely to succeed in your job and continue to stay on track in other areas as well.

Medication may not be for everyone. For me, my life didn't start turning around for the good until I found a medication that worked for me. It took several tries to find an appropriate fit. Don't give up too soon and don't change from one to another too quickly, as either method could cause you to fail before you have even given them a fair shot.

If you have too many medications in your system at once, the ADHD symptoms can be acerbated rather than subdued. Make sure to give your body time to completely eliminate one before trying another. Once you start taking medication, it doesn't mean that you will be on it for the rest of your life. Once you learn how to get your life in order through different methods, you may then be able to stop taking them.

Life Coach

The busy lifestyles of people today have helped to develop a whole new career option for those who "have it all together." The life coach gets paid to tell people like us how we can be more productive with simple changes in the way we do things on a daily basis. I realize that not everyone can afford to hire a life coach, or you may live in an area where they have not even heard of them yet. If you followed the suggestion earlier in the book, you should at least have a support system at hand. They, too, may not be very organized, but they can help you find someone who is, or encourage you while you utilize the following suggestions to help you get started.

Calendar

A calendar can be a very helpful tool for someone who has ADHD. Office supply stores usually carry very large calendars with lots of room to write for each day. I would highly suggest purchasing one of these calendars and hanging it on a wall where it can be plainly seen every day. These calendars are typically made to go on a desk, but if you hang it on the wall, it is more visible and less likely to get covered up by something else.

The next step is to get in the habit of writing on it and checking it regularly. This may not sound like much, but it wouldn't hurt to have someone help you with this. Have them meet with you at a certain time each day so you can go over your schedule together. The end of the day is probably the best time for this. You can use this opportunity to add any appointments that you may have made during the day and check to see what is going on the next day so you can be prepared.

If you have any appointments scheduled that require you to do something in advance, such as request time off work, get a babysitter, call your car pool and let them know you won't be able to drive that day, etc., schedule when you plan to do those things as well. I have a health condition that requires that I take an antibiotic before I get my teeth cleaned. The dentist's receptionist calls the prescription in to the pharmacy for me, and I have to make sure I pick it up. If I am scheduled to have my teeth cleaned at 8:00, and the pharmacy doesn't open until 9:00, I make sure to write on the calendar that I have to pick up my prescription on the day before I go to the dentist.

If you decide to take a prescription for ADHD, chances are it may be a controlled substance. These prescriptions cannot be phoned in to the pharmacy. You must bring in a hand written copy from your doctor every month. It is a good idea to write in when you plan to call your doctor to order the prescription every month, as some doctors require a twenty-four to forty-eight hour advance notice for this. Then write in the day you plan to pick it up and have it filled.

In addition to writing in special occasions such as birthdays and anniversaries, you can also write in a day to pick up a card or gift as well so you don't get caught by surprise. Basically, write in everything that is important to remember and everything that goes with it as well. If you tend to arrive late for everything, you can even go so far as to change the times for your appointments to be a little early. For example, if you have an appointment with your doctor at 11:45, write it down as 11:30 instead to give yourself a little breathing room.

Get Organized

By knowing what characteristics you have that are most likely caused by ADHD, you can begin to tackle them one at a time. If, for example, you are always misplacing things, there are steps you can take to create a more organized environment. To begin with, less is more. In other words, the less you have, the more often you will find what you are looking for!

It can be difficult to part with personal possessions for some people. It is important to remember that a little discomfort now will make your life a lot more comfortable later. Any item you choose to keep must meet at least one of these criteria: either it must be used regularly, or be of considerable sentimental value. Again, I will stress that you should have a person from your support system on hand during this time. When you get to a point where you are slowing down, or letting items slip by that don't meet the criteria, they can remind you and encourage you to keep going.

This first step is crucial to becoming more organized. You need to be able to work with the space you have available. Once you have eliminated the things that are merely clutter, you can begin with the next step. Each item that has met the criteria and you will be keeping must then be given a specific spot where it will be kept. At this point, I can only give basic suggestions about how you will do this because each person's items, homes, and lifestyles will vary.

Car keys are an item that many tend to misplace. A hook on the wall next to the door is a perfect spot where they can be hung up upon arriving home and quickly grabbed on the way out. Location is vital in making sure that each item gets put back in its home after each use. It would be pointless to keep your reading glasses on the shelf over the kitchen sink, for example, when the only time you read is in bed. Keep the item where you use it most.

If mail tends to get lost or covered up in one of the many piles before you have a chance to go through it, bills may not get paid on time. If this is a problem for you, create a place specifically for mail right inside the entrance door. Use this spot for just mail. It could be a mail organizer hung on the wall where you can separate bills from junk mail, or each person's mail could be separated if others live with you. It could be as easy as just hanging a basket on the wall where all of the mail can be placed until you have a chance to go through it.

I cannot possibly tell you what to do with every item in your home. Think about how, when, and where you use each item and create a spot for it accordingly. Storage containers come in a variety of sizes and styles that can be filled, labeled, and stored neatly in a closet or under a bed. I like to use large colored totes for storage. A variety of colors can be purchased for different occasions or each member of the family to have a color of their own. I use red totes for Christmas decorations, and when my children were younger, they each got a different color tote to store their things in so I could tell which tote belonged to whom without having to open it up.

There was a time when it was my mission to have everything organized. When I felt like my life was falling apart, downsizing and organizing everything I owned made me feel like I at least had control over something. If organizing your home sounds like too much for you to tackle right away, start with you car, desk, or even your purse first. As you start to get the hang of it and see how much easier it is to keep track of what you have, you can begin to work on your home by focusing on one room at a time.

I have seen shows on television where people remove everything from the house and divide it into sections on the lawn marked keep, sell, and throw away. They are then only allowed to bring back inside the items that they intend to keep. This requires having someone to supervise and a team to help pull it off. I would not recommend doing something of this magnitude on your own. You may very well end up with all of your possessions left sitting in the yard covered up by a tarp. It may takes weeks or even months of you peeking under the tarp in your pajamas every morning, trying to find something to wear to work before you finally get back around to finishing the job.

If you must do the organizing by yourself, or even if

you have another person or two that will help, focus on completing one room at a time. Notice I said "completing." I have been known to get tired of one room and start on another just for a change of scenery. The only thing this does is make it necessary for me to restart the original room from the beginning at a later date.

Have a garbage can nearby so you can immediately pitch items that you have no use for. If you simply put them in a pile to throw away later, you may end up having to go through that same pile again someday. Have boxes on hand to put items in that you plan to get rid of. If you are going to be having a yard sale so you can sell your treasures, you can label and store the boxes until you have finished with all of the rooms. On the other hand, if you plan to donate the unwanted items to a local charity or second hand store, try to drop off the boxes periodically. This accomplishes two things; it will prevent you from going back through the boxes and pulling items out later, and it will be a lot easier on the people who are receiving your donation as they won't have as many boxes to go through at once.

After removing all of the trash and unnecessary items, gather the remaining articles together. Some things that are very important to consider when deciding how your storage system will be set up is how often each item will be used and which items are used together. Any item that is used rather frequently should be stored in a place that is accessed easily and items that are used together should be stored together if possible to prevent them from getting separated.

If you have to get on your knees and pull a box out from under your bed every day just to find a pair of shoes, for example, chances are, those shoes are not going to get put back into the box after awhile because it is just too much of an inconvenience. Perhaps a shoe organizer that hangs on the inside of your closet door would be a much better choice. This does not mean that you can't use the under-the-bed shoe storage unit. You might want to use it for your off-season shoes instead. You can then rotate the pairs of shoes from the hanging shoe organizer to the box under the bed at the end of each season when you have no plans on wearing them again for awhile.

You will be able to have more clothes and keep your closet less cluttered by doing the same thing with your wardrobe. Seasonal clothes can be stored outside of your closet, making it much easier to find what you are looking for on a day-to-day basis. Most of us have clothes that we don't wear because they are too small. We are sure that with a little motivation we will be able to fit back into them someday. Some life coaches might tell you to get rid of them and if you do lose the weight, you can treat yourself to some new clothes. That sounds great, and if you can afford a life coach, you could probably afford to purchase a new wardrobe too.

Realistically, if it is a mere twenty pounds or so that is keeping you from wearing those clothes, and it hasn't been that long since you did wear them, you may want to simply remove them from your closet and store them in a safe place instead. This will free up space for what you are currently wearing and prevent you from having to reinvest in more clothes later. It is not uncommon for people to start feeling better about themselves after getting their lives more organized. Once you finish going through all of the rooms in your house, you may find that you are motivated enough to lose that weight after all.

Parenting with ADHD

Undoing Years of Frustration

Learning to adjust to a personal diagnosis of ADHD can be difficult. When you have children to care for it can be even more challenging. To top it off, most likely, one or more of your children have it as well. While one might think that this would make dealing with your newfound diagnosis more difficult, most likely you have already been dealing with your child's disorder for some time now and this will simply shed light on why you have been having such a difficult time getting them organized. Learning that you and your child both have the same challenges can actually make it easier for you to help them as well as yourself.

By helping your child to understand what ADHD is and that it is in no way a defect of their character, you will be reinforcing this in your own mind as well. When learning how to be more successful in daily life, a child may feel less "abnormal" if they are sharing their progress and struggles with a parent who also has ADHD. By checking in with each other throughout the day, staying on track could be much easier for both of you. You may find that the discovery of ADHD in yourself, and the awareness that goes with it, could be all you need to turn the stumbling blocks of yesterday into the stepping stones of tomorrow.

Parenting Classes

Parenting classes are available through different government agencies. Check with your local Human Services Agency to see what is available to you. These classes are set up to teach parents what to expect from their children at the different stages of life and the best ways to handle conflict as it arises during each stage. They can even provide information about parenting children with ADHD and other learning disabilities.

Chances are, if you have ADHD, you have been very frustrated in your role as a parent. Consistency is crucial when raising children, and consistency is not always a strong point in people with ADHD. Children do best when they know where their boundaries are. If the rules keep changing, it makes it easier for them to mess up, and we want our children to succeed. Too many rules, even while consistent, can trip up our children as well. Decide what rules are necessary and what the punishment will be for breaking those rules. If you don't enforce the punishment consistently, the child may start to think that they don't need to follow the rules consistently either.

An example of this that comes to mind is when parents have a hard time keeping their children in their car seats. I am referring to children who are old enough to know better. When a toddler figures out how to escape from their car seat, and they usually will, if the parent tells them to stay in their seat, then does nothing about it when they don't, this could become a problem down the road ... literally.

It may be hard to gauge when to be consistent and when to allow for some spontaneity. If a rule is set up for safety reasons, such as staying in their car seat, no exceptions should ever be made. Otherwise, occasional exceptions could be made. An example of this would be chores that a child is required to do. If a chore is to be done at a certain time each day, such as dishes that get washed right after dinner; don't make your child miss out on a special opportunity that arises simply out of formality. Instead, allow your child to be creative and come up with an alternative. He could offer to switch chores with another sibling, possibly doing extra chores for them out of gratitude, or they may ask you to wash them in exchange for washing your car. This will not only prevent your child from having to miss out on something that they would get a lot of enjoyment out of, but it helps them learn how to work out a compromise with others and how to adjust to life's sudden changes.

Classes are available that can teach a parent how to set up age appropriate expectations for all of their children. As they mature, the rules and consequences also need to change. Most parents would like to believe that all they need are good instincts to raise their children, and for the most part that would be true. There is nothing wrong with seeking out assistance when you find yourself overwhelmed and at a loss for what to do next.

School Programs

Your special needs child has services available to them at school if requested by you. Many times a teacher will approach the parent about these services when they detect a problem. If you already know that your child has ADHD, you can approach the school about these services before any problems begin. By utilizing these tools ahead of time, it can keep your child on track so it doesn't get overwhelming for them. This will also take some of the pressure off of you, as your child will have someone at school that is making sure that they are completing their work and getting it turned in on time.

You may have a hard time accepting this help, let alone requesting it. As the parent, it may be so engrained in your mind that you are the one responsible for doing these things, that you turn away an opportunity for your child to do their best out of stubborn pride. I had a difficult time keeping track of what my children were supposed to be doing in school and I thought it was great when I found out about the programs available to them. Unfortunately, this didn't happen until my last child was a junior in high school.

These programs don't have to be an "all or nothing" deal either. Just because a program offers certain services, doesn't mean that you have to take them all. When my daughter joined the resource room at her high school, I learned that the kids using that room were allowed to use their notes during tests, while other kids were not. My daughter had a difficult time concentrating when taking a test and she typically needed extra time. She was able to get that by taking her tests in the resource room, but I did not want her to use her notes if the rest of her class could not. After all, she was being tested on what she had learned, not on how well she could take notes. Discuss what services are available and make sure you let the instructor know which ones you want your child to participate in.

Parenting ADHD vs. Non-ADHD Children

When parenting children who have ADHD as well as those who don't, the differences between them can be obvious. For that matter, all children in the same family can be very different too, whether ADHD is a factor at all. As much as parents may try to treat their children the same, there really isn't anything wrong with treating them differently. Sure, you want to love them all the same and offer them all the same opportunities, but they are different and with their different personalities come different needs, different strengths and different weaknesses. We as parents need to keep this in mind when dealing with our children so we can help each of them become the best person they can be.

Don't give one child a hard time because they don't get all "A's" like another one does. As long as you can see that each is doing the best that they can do, and are being given the necessary tools in which to do that, grades should not be the only measurement for success that you use with your children. As each child moves past their own personal hurtles in life, they should be given the credit due to them.

While the same rules apply to all of the children,

some may need more guidance or assistance with following them than others. This theory can go the other direction as well. Just because one child requires more help than another, that does not mean that you should provide that same help to all of your children. If you know that they are capable of performing well without it; it would actually be to their disadvantage to make things easier for them.

Social Skills

The tendency for a person with ADHD to be impulsive, restless, forgetful, and unable to focus can put them at a big disadvantage in social situations. When a person keeps losing track of what others are saying, doesn't pay attention to what is going on around them, and keeps interrupting the conversation, they may end up feeling rather foolish, or at least looking that way to others because they may not even realize what they are doing is wrong.

Those with ADHD may not be able to read people well or have good social graces. Explain to your child about taking turns in conversation, keeping their voice low in certain situations, how to ask appropriate questions, being discrete, etc. This may not seem like much, but it could mean the difference between your children having a healthy social circle, versus them living a very lonely life. Most likely, if you have ADHD too, social skills may not be your best asset either and by teaching these things to your child, you will be able to reinforce them with yourself as well.

Break Down Tasks

Some problems can seem so insurmountable to a child with ADHD that they don't know where to begin. Cleaning her bedroom was like this for my daughter. She could sit on the floor of her room with a blank stare on her face for two hours not knowing where to begin. I would have to practically hand her each item and tell her where to put it.

At the time, we didn't know she had ADHD. For that matter, I didn't know I had it either. But, I was creative and I did come up with a solution that helped with the room cleaning dilemma for many years. I made drawstring bags out of printed material. The pictures on each bag were of the things that should go into that bag. All of her little people went in the bag with the pictures of people on it; the animals went into the bag with the pictures of animals on it; blocks with blocks, etc. Then I put hooks on the wall to hang the bags on. Instead of my daughter sitting there feeling overwhelmed by all of the toys in front of her, she would grab a bag and try to find all of the items in her room that went in that bag. She continued this until all that was left were clothes and stuffed animals, etc. These items, too, had their own place to go and were much more manageable once the rest was cleared away.

When my kids were old enough to prepare food for themselves I would often come home to find the kitchen sink full of dirty dishes left behind from the preparation of someone's culinary creation. Doing dishes was a chore that they typically took turns with, so inevitably, one child would prepare a meal using every pan in the kitchen when it was someone else's week to wash the dishes. They would then refrain from cooking during their own week. This particular chore was one that everyone disliked. Hours might go by when one of my children with ADHD had to take their turn. It seemed overwhelming to them and I would get frustrated every time I had to redirect them back to the sink.

Someone came up with a wonderful invention to wash dishes. They put a sponge on the end of a tube and filled the tube with dish soap. The soap comes out of a hole and goes into the sponge which is then used to wash dishes. The length of the tube allows the sponge to reach down into glasses for easy cleaning. This tool makes it possible to wash dishes as they accumulate rather than waiting until you have a whole sink full. I was able to use this invention to solve a problem in my home.

I got tired of trying to monitor who was dirtying too many dishes and who was responsible for washing them. I bought one of those sponges on a stick and told my kids that they were each responsible for washing their own dishes with it. Even after a meal, as each child brought their dishes to the kitchen sink, they were required to wash their plate, silverware, and glass with the soapy wand, rinse, and place them in the dish drainer. Whoever cooked the meal was then responsible for washing the pots and pans.

Parenting Today vs. Previous Generations

There are a lot of differences in the way children are raised today in comparison to what I experienced as a child. I was born in the early sixties; for the most part, I had a fairly simple childhood: better than some, worse than others. I was never without anything that I truly needed, and I was spoiled from time to time. I was expected to be respectful and follow the rules or my father's belt would come off. Yet, I had the freedom to use my imagination and explore the world and all it had to offer. In other words, I was told to go outside and play. That was typical back then, and I'm glad that it was. It gave me a lot of wonderful memories.

I believe the time and place that I grew up in made it easier for me to deal with ADHD as a child. Even though I did injure myself quite often, I managed to do okay otherwise. Whereas most kids today always have something to keep them occupied, such as television or video games, the majority of my days were spent exploring and learning from hands on experiences that enhanced my imagination.

I'm not saying my parents never gave us anything fun to do. We went camping, fishing, and snowmobiling. I had an awesome playhouse that my dad made for me. It was big enough for adults to stand up in, with real windows and a covered front porch. My dad made a track in the field behind our house for my brothers and me to ride our little motorcycle around. We also had a small hobby farm with a variety of animals. Childhood was good!

We weren't rich by any means, but my parents were resourceful. The snowmobile and motorcycle weren't new and my parents worked hard and did a lot of things themselves. Mom worked from home doing odd jobs, so she was always there when we needed her. She made a lot of my clothes and grew a lot of our food.

ADHD children do well when they are given a good

mixture of time with and without structure. They need to have a lot of room for creativity, yet their boundaries should be clear and enforced. I feel very blessed to have had the childhood I had. It provided all of these things.

Even my father's intimidating punishments played a part in keeping my ADHD in check. Spanking may be taboo today because we have learned better ways to correct a child, but when I was growing up, it was the norm. I may have stayed out of trouble out of fear of my father... but I stayed out of trouble! I'm sure the years of therapy I went through to find out why I was continually drawn to controlling men had nothing to do with that.

By the time I reached my teen years, I was becoming a self-absorbed, hormonal pain in the neck. ADHD tends to make people very emotional. The changes my body was going through added to that, making me overly dramatic about everything. My poor mom had to listen to so much. At least I think she was listening; some evenings, while she was making dinner, I would hide under the table and go on and on to her about how difficult my life was. I can't recall ever getting any major responses from her though. I do remember telling her once, "Someday, when I have a daughter and she's this age, I'm going to remember what this feels like and I'm going to take pity on her!"

Looking back, my mom had the right idea. I did take pity on my daughter when she was "suffering" at that age. I ended up making things worse for her too. I tried to fight her battles, and in turn, all I did was humiliate her even more. I think parents today feel compelled to try and make things easier for their children. Whether it is because we remember what it was like for us at that age, as I did, or because the high divorce rate has caused the family to be in such disarray that we feel we owe it to them. Often times, we are just making it more difficult for them in the long run. Even children who have the added stress of ADHD need to learn how to handle their own battles when they are young so they will be able to handle the larger ones as they get older.

I was fortunate enough to have a very strict father who thought I could do anything. I never dreamed I would ever be saying that. I used to think he was too hard on me, and that he didn't approve of me. When he would say, "You can do that," I thought he was pushing me and expecting more than I was capable of. He didn't say it in an encouraging way. It felt almost like he was appalled that I hadn't already succeeded. It wasn't until well after his death, when I was a lot older, that I realized he wasn't just saying that to get me to try harder. He really did think I could do anything. If he was appalled when he said it, he was more than likely appalled that I didn't realize it too. He apparently would brag to others about me and the things I had done. I just don't remember him ever telling me that I did a great job on anything. He did tell me that he loved me ... once. That I will never forget.

I have always taken everything so personally. People with ADHD don't always see the other person's side of a situation. They tend to only see themselves and how they feel, and often get defensive if someone questions what they are doing or how they are doing it. If I say "hello" to someone and they seem distracted, I automatically think they are mad at me. When my dad's behavior toward me started changing as I got older, I automatically thought that I had done something wrong. I failed to even try to see his view of the situation.

My dad grew up during a time when men didn't express their feelings. I knew he loved me when I was a little girl. He had a way with kids; he loved to play and have fun. It was the serious stuff that he had a hard time with; the kind of stuff a girl starts dealing with by her early teen years. I started to think that he didn't love me anymore. I misinterpreted his suggestions for me as disappointment in what I was doing. Unfortunately, he died when I was nineteen. I was just getting to the age where I was old enough and confident enough to start having adult conversations with him. What we probably could have hashed out together over a six month period, took me about twenty years to figure out on my own.

These days, communication is highly valued and encouraged for men as well as women. People make a point of spending quality time with their children of all ages and everyone's feelings are important. Whereas years ago, women had to beat around the bush and guess what men were thinking about, now men are grilled regularly and are becoming fairly proficient at using "I" statements. By the time today's young boys are fathers, it should be a second language for them. As all children are taught to express their feelings, those with ADHD will benefit from not only learning to communicate their thoughts in a productive way, but they will also be made aware that others have feelings as well. Maybe they won't be as likely to take another person's behavior so personally.

A child's social life is taken a lot more seriously these days. Parents feel more compelled than ever to encourage their children to participate in a wide range of extra-curricular activities. This adds a whole new dimension to a person's day planner when each child has to be at a different location at the same time. When I was a kid, if we wanted to do something, we got the neighbors together for a game of Kick-the-Can or Red Rover. This isn't always practical anymore. While my mom stayed home with us, parents can't be home as often anymore. The streets are getting more and more dangerous for kids, and a dance class, hockey team, or drama club can be a safe haven for a child.

It is always important to give a child with ADHD some down time to choose from non-structured activities, but sometimes societal pressures cause parents to overload their child's schedule. They may want them to have everything that the Jones's kids have. I felt a lot of pressure over the years to keep my children involved in certain sports. Some can be very time consuming. I remember one particular year when all three of my children played hockey. That season I spent as many as twenty hours a week at the rink. Don't get me wrong, I love to watch my kids have fun as much as any parent does, but I sure could have used that extra time to catch up on things, and rushing from rink to rink took a toll on me.

My children's father felt very strongly that the kids play hockey. The equipment and the fee to join were costly enough, and then there were things to sell on top of it to raise extra money for the association. The weekend tournaments required time off work as well as money for gas, food, and hotel rooms. I am by no means a sports fan and my budget was tight enough as it was. Hockey was not a necessity, so I refused to pay the entrance fee or buy expensive equipment, but I would help sell whatever they were required to sell, and I would take turns bringing them to their practices and games, including the out-of-town tournaments.

The point I am trying to make is that my experience with hockey is just one example of how stressful people's lives are becoming. It's burdensome not having enough time or money to cover what a family needs just to get by, but then we feel pressure from factors outside and inside the family structure to do things that further stress our mental and monetary capacity, as well as our moral being. We have to keep redefining our boundaries. Time and money are stretched so far that we end up giving up things that are important to us like church, a family vacation, or just a good quality meal at a fancy restaurant.

Parenting is something that will continue to evolve and change as society changes. This makes debating which generation has or had better parenting techniques irrelevant. Each generation has its own trials and complications to deal with. As long as parents have the best interest of their children in mind, no matter who has ADHD; that is the most important thing.

ADHD and Marriage

When Both Partners Have ADHD

When two people with ADHD get married, the outcome could be rather unpredictable. If both of them are impulsive, lousy at handling finances, keep an unorganized home, and abuse alcohol, for example, they may become more frustrated when their previous lifestyle difficulties are intensified with the other person's additional baggage. On the other hand, since they both have the same pitfalls, they may be able to empathize with each other and become even closer because of it. It could end up being a very dysfunctional, yet happy marriage that lasts for fifty or so unproductive years. It all depends on how you look at it.

On the other hand, if one of the partners is trying to control their ADHD by taking medication and focusing on getting organized, they may find that they are continuously getting set back in their progress. They may even have to work twice as hard in order to make up for their spouse's lack of order. The amount of stress one may experience when trying to regain control in their life is already significant enough without having to also pick up the pieces of someone else's mistakes and mayhem.

Be Patient with Your Partner

Since ADHD has not been associated with adults for very long now, there are many who have a hard time even believing that it is a real issue. If you are an adult with ADHD who is married to a person like this, you may be in for a very bumpy ride. I had initially meant for this section to be about being patient with your non-ADHD partner, but it really goes both ways.

Communication is key in making a marriage work, whether ADHD is an issue or not. Each person needs to let the other one know where they stand and then both parties need to put forth an effort to make sure that the other person's interests are kept in mind. If people in marriages were more concerned about making sure that their spouse was getting everything that they need out of the marriage, there would be a lot less divorce. In order for this to work, they both have to be looking out for the other one. If only one of them is, while the other is looking out for number one, someone is going to feel short changed eventually.

Just because a person has ADHD does not mean that they get to use that as an excuse to get out of doing work. I would hope that anyone who chooses to read this book is doing so out of the desire to find answers as to how they can improve their lives and be a more pro-ductive member of their family and society in general. I did not write this book to give people an excuse for not trying, rather so they may be able to identify why they have been struggling. Knowledge gives you power. Once the source of the problem is properly addressed, it can be properly dealt with.

Both parties in a marriage need to allow the other room to adjust. Sit down and identify problems that the other may not even be aware of. If, for example, the spouse with ADHD is told they don't seem to listen very well, they can try to break down the problem to find a solution. Perhaps the ADHD spouse gets too absorbed in their thoughts and doesn't always realize that they are being told something. A solution for this could be for their spouse to always make sure to get their attention before they pass along information. Once they make sure the ADHD spouse is looking at them and paying attention, then they can continue. To make sure that important details are not missed or misunderstood, the non-ADHD spouse could mention that it is very important that they hear this, and then have the ADHD spouse repeat what they are told to make sure there is no misunderstanding. This may seem foolish and unnecessary, but many people holler out across rooms, or over loud noises, and then don't stick around long enough to make sure the message was received. If the person receiving the information has ADHD, they may not even realize someone was talking to them in the first place.

Your Partner's Emotional Well-Being

I'm certain that I've read somewhere that after being married to a person with ADHD, a non-ADHD person tends to develop psychological disorders. I warned my husband about this when he proposed to me, but he married me anyway! I can see where an otherwise sane person could begin to develop mental health issues after being married to someone who has a lot of ADHD tendencies, but, I believe that the tables can get turned when a person with ADHD marries someone with control issues. There are way too many personality types, and possible combinations of these types in marriages, to make a concrete judgment like that. It can go both ways.

Imagine if a person without ADHD, who was used to having things neat and organized, preferred to follow a regular routine, and had an impressive credit score, married someone with ADHD who let things pile up in total disarray, flew through life without any structure, and was avoiding calls from the creditors due to outstanding bills. I see a few possible scenarios coming out of a union like that.

If the non-ADHD partner is passive and doesn't like confrontation and the partner with ADHD is bold and controlling, this could end up very badly for the non-ADHD spouse. Without having the gumption necessary to confront their spouse and work out their differences, he or she would most likely find themselves living in a world that goes totally against the way they prefer to live. They may begin to shy away from their friends and family out of embarrassment and fear that someone may come to their home and see the conditions that they live in. They may be the one who finds the need to hide an elephant rather than the spouse with ADHD. If their spouse with ADHD continues to set them back due to his or her irresponsible financial practices, the dreams that they had for the future could quickly disappear. The non-ADHD spouse could very well begin to suffer from anxiety or depression caused by the lack of control they feel they have in their life.

If the non-ADHD partner is the bold and controlling one, and the ADHD partner is more passive, it could be the spouse with ADHD who has a harder time adjusting. The spouse without ADHD would most likely have no problem forcing the issues they have with their partner's lack of organization and structure. This pressure would most likely cause the spouse with ADHD to have a more difficult time keeping things in order. This, in turn, might cause their controlling spouse to be even more critical of them. The passive spouse with ADHD could very well be the one who develops the anxiety and depression described earlier.

I believe the second scenario is more dangerous than the first. The non-ADHD passive spouse may feel they don't have control of their home life, but they do have control over their own actions. If they were to leave the relationship, they can recapture the structure they so desire. After all, it was the other person's actions that caused their world to fall apart, not their own. If the passive spouse who has ADHD were to leave the relationship, provided they had enough self-confidence left to leave, they would leave feeling like a failure. They would have been told over and over that they weren't good enough. It can be hard to pick yourself up and start over when you feel like this.

The last two scenarios are pretty typical. Most people see things from their own viewpoint and fail to try the other person's shoes on, or they are so set on seeking peace and approval that the stress finally gets the better of them. It really should not matter what personalities the couple have, as long as they take the time to communicate their feelings and respect each other's opinion. The ADHD spouse may be able to get the non-ADHD spouse to relax their rigid schedule a little bit, allowing them to experience things they would never allow themselves to experience before. The spouse with ADHD, by taking tips from their non-ADHD spouse, may learn to be more productive, allowing them to be spontaneous without the usual guilt of not having things completed. Opposites are said to attract. With communication and respect, they can learn to live together peacefully as well.

Financial Responsibilities

Many people with ADHD find themselves in financial difficulties due to their forgetfulness, poor organizational skills, and impulsivity. On the other hand, just because a person doesn't have ADHD, that doesn't mean that they will be good at handling finances either. In light of this fact, it may not be in the best interest of a marriage for a spouse to be left in charge of the financial responsibilities simply because they are the one who doesn't have ADHD.

With all of the technological advances that we enjoy today (and I use the word "enjoy" loosely here) there are more ways than ever for a person to keep track of their finances and make their payments on time. Many employers offer electronic deposit to their employees. With this service, a person's pay check can be automatically deposited into one or several different accounts of the employees choosing. By not having to handle their check, a person can avoid the pitfalls that they may typically be confronted with. Here are some advantages of this, as well as other, automatic electronic transactions:

1. You don't have to worry about losing or misplacing your check.

2. You don't have to try and remember to stop at the bank.

3. Payments for loans can be set up to come out of your account automatically. You won't have to try and remember when payments are due, or make a special trip to the bank to make them.

4. Most types of bills can be set up to come out of your checking account or be charged to your credit card automatically. This will help you avoid late payments and possible disconnections that come along with more fees to reinstate your service.

5. You can have your credit card payment made automatically every month. Set it up to pay the minimum payment, the entire balance, or an amount of your choice.

6. Overdraft charges on a checking account can add up quickly due to one simple error on your part that causes a check to bounce. It is a good idea to get overdraft protection to prevent this from happening.

As long as your income covers all of your payments and everything is set up to happen automatically, you shouldn't have to worry about getting behind on payments, having utilities disconnected, or being charged extra fees for mistakes that you might make.

Famous People
with ADHD

I find it encouraging to hear about others who have been diagnosed with ADHD and still manage to be successful. Sometimes, I believe it is the positive ADHD symptoms that actually help cause their success, despite the negative symptoms. I have come across the names of several famous people who are said to have had ADHD. The majority of them are people who could never have actually been diagnosed with it, as they were deceased before the diagnostic process even began. Some people in the public eye today appear to have ADHD from the way they behave. I was able to find a few who had been diagnosed and publicly admit to this diagnosis.

Olympic swimmer, Michael Phelps, apparently was diagnosed with ADHD at a young age. His story was chronicled in the Baltimore Sun by Kevin Van Valkenburg on August 3, 2008. Swimming became an outlet for his excess energy and led to his recent fame. That fame, in turn, then put him on a pedestal for all to see when he made an impulsive decision that put him in a negative light as well. When Michael was at a party, he gave in to peer pressure and took part in recreational drug use. A picture of this was unknowingly captured and released to the press. He admitted to doing what the picture claimed and apologized for the poor example he had set for his young fans, but his career still suffered some major blemishes because of it.

Certain responsibilities come from being an Olympic gold medal winner. There are a lot of children who look up to him as a role model. This was probably not something that he really thought about when he joined the Olympic team, or when he was doing drugs for that matter, but the parents of those children take it very seriously. They probably held Michael up as a shining example of hard work and discipline, and then were left speechless when the news of his indiscretion came out. This created another lesson altogether for their children to learn. I would like to think that the parents explained to their children that Michael made a mistake, admitted to it, and apologized. This does not make him a bad person; he just did a bad thing. If we make mistakes in life, what matters most is that we humbly accept the consequences for our actions then continue to keep striving to be the best that we can be. If I were in his shoes, I would probably have crawled under a rock somewhere and never shown my face again. It took a lot of courage for him to handle it in the way that he did. It does not make what he did any better or "okay" by any means, but he is not allowing that one lapse in good judgment to cripple him or hold him back. By this, he has set a good example for those of us with ADHD as well.

Many times I have made the assumption that one actor or another must have ADHD. The over-the-top manner in which Robin Williams and Jim Carrey present themselves, for example, could easily be written off as them having this diagnosis. It wouldn't be out of line to say that it is the creative, artistic, exuberant way in which many actors present themselves that make them so valuable in their line of work. Since it is these qualities which also tend to show up in people who have ADHD, it makes it appear as though most successful actors must have it too.

Howie Mandell has publicly admitted to having this disorder. He is currently doing advertising for a campaign called "ADHD is real." Ty Pennington of ABC's Extreme Home Makeover does commercials for a prescription medication and tells how it has helped him to control his ADHD. As much trouble as this condition may have given these people, it can most likely be attributed to their success as well.

Albert Einstein, Walt Disney, Alexander Graham Bell, and Thomas Edison are all believed to have had ADHD. I imagine it is the exciting way in which each of them has made a major impact on the world with their ability to "think outside of the box" that has brought people to this conclusion. ADHD comes with a lot of good qualities. People tend to be drawn to us for our excitable, empathetic, and loving nature. Others are inspired by us because of the intelligent, inventive ways in which we envision new possibilities. Still more are captivated by the original, artistic ways in which we use our creativity to make the world a more beautiful place.

I wanted to end my book with this chapter because I believe that people with ADHD don't always believe that they can amount to much. They get frustrated with the struggle that becomes a part of their daily life and end up expecting less and less of themselves because of it. It doesn't have to be that way. By following the details laid out in these pages, a person can learn which characteristics they have that can be attributed to ADHD and how to go about dealing with them. Through treatment, therapy, education or a combination of these things a person can become a more effective parent, spouse, or person in general. Use this information to help you locate the tools you have at your disposal. You are not alone.

The most important thing to remember is that ADHD is not something to be ashamed of. A person does not need to hide this disorder from the world. The more society learns about ADHD and what goes along with it, the better we will all be. Knowledge is power; so become empowered. After reading the characteristics described in this book, if you think you may have ADHD, get tested. Once diagnosed, a person can begin to see that there is a very good reason they have been struggling through life. This realization can be the beginning to a whole new outlook and the courage to start making changes for the better. The steps necessary to start living the life you have dreamed of are in your hands; not only in spite of, but because of having ADHD as well.

While having ADHD had challenged me to the point of breaking, it has made me a stronger person. While it had cast me into darkness, it has helped me to see God's light shine that much brighter. While it had made me hate myself, it has made me more sensitive toward others. The struggles I have endured because of this disorder have made me a much better person than I ever would have been without it.

Lightning Source UK Ltd.
Milton Keynes UK
UKOW04f1231280115

245269UK00001B/83/P